WEATHER
Snow 32
Rain 32
Rainbows 33
Sun 33
Sunrise/Sunset 33
Clouds 33

SPORTS & OUTDOOR ACTIVITIES
General 34
Archery 34
Baseball 34
Basketball 35
Bicycling 35
Boxing 35
Cheerleading 35
Fishing 35
Flying Kites 36
Football 36
Golf 36
Gymnastics 37
Hiking 37
Hockey 37
Hunting 37
Rafting 38
Skating 38
Skiing 38
Soccer 38
Surfing 38
Tennis 39
Track/Running 39
Volleyball 39
Walking 39
Wrestling 39

SCHOOL DAYS
School 40
Teachers 40
Teenagers 41
Apples 41
Graduation 42
Art 42
Bus 43
College 43
Computers 43
Prom 43

PETS, ANIMALS & INSECTS
General 44
Ants 44
Bear 44
Bee 44
Bird 45
Bugs 45
Butterfly 45
Cats 45
Chicken 46
Cow 46
Dogs 46
Ducks 47
Frog 47
Horse 47
Mice 47
Monkey 47
Pig 48
Rabbit 48
Sheep 48
Snakes 48
Spider 48
Worm 48

FARMING & RANCHING
Farm 49
Ranch 49

FOOD, DIET & EXERCISE
Eating 50
Baking & Cooking 50
Diet & Exercise 51

THIS 'N THAT
Acting 52
Angels 52
Bath Time 52
Bedtime 53
Cameras 53
Church & Religion 53
Death 54
Driving 54
Eyeglasses 54
Fire 54
Firsts 54
Flowers & Garden 54
Gambling 55
Boy & Girl Scouts 56
Hair 56
Happy 56
House & Home 56
Injury, Illness & Hospital 56
Inspirational 57
Love, Kisses & Hearts 58
Memories 59
Messy 59
Military 60
Miscellaneous 60
Money 60
Music, Dance & Show Business 60
Motorcycle 61
Newspaper 61
Noah's Ark 61
Reunions 61
Sad 61
Shopping 62
Sleeping 62
Stars 62
Teeth 62
Telephone 63
Time 63
Toilet & Toilet Training 63
Trains 63
Tree House 63
Trouble 63
Under Construction 64
Volunteer 64
Working World 64
World 64
Wreck 64

Family & Special People

FAMILY, HERITAGE & TRADITIONS

A Classic
A Family Affair
A Family That Prays Together Stays Together
A Timeless Treasure
A Visit Inside Our Home
All in the Family
An Annual Event
Beauty from the Past
Bits of Yesterday
Cherished Days
Crossing Paths
Deep Rooted Heritage
Faces from the Past
Faces of Our Family
Families are Forever
Family Matters
Family Portrait
Family Ties
Family Tradition
From Days Gone By
From Past to Present
Generation Gap
Generation to Generation
Generations
God Bless Our Home
Gone But Never Forgotten
Home Sweet Home
I Remember When...
If We Could Freeze Time...
It All Starts and Ends with Family
Leave Your Mark
Magical Memories
Making History
Memories
Memories for a Lifetime
Memory Lane
My Ancestors
My Heritage
Obviously, Good Looks Run in the Family
Once Upon a Lifetime...
Once Upon a Time...
One Big Happy Family
Our Clan
Our Family is a Circle of Love
Our Legacy
Remember When...
Remember Your Roots
Same Time, Same Place, Different Year
Seems Like Yesterday
Step Back into Time
The Clan
The Good Ol' Days
The Good Old Days
The Passage of Time
The Ties That Bind a Family Together
The Way It Was
The Way We Were
Then and Now
These are the Times to Remember

Those Were the Days
Through the Years
Timeless Treasures
Travel Back in Time
Treasured Memories
Treasured Thoughts
We are a Happy Family
We are Family
We Begin and End with Family
Welcome to Our Funny Farm
Where Did the Time Go?
Yesteryear

....

....

....

....

....

....

PARENTS

"M" is for Mom
"M" is for Mom, not Maid
A Mom of All Trades
A Mother is a Girl's Best Friend
A Mother's Touch
A Mother's Work is Never Done
A Very Special Mom
Always Caring and Always Giving
Dad is the Best
Dads are Great!
Dad's Corner
Dad's Fix-it Shop
Daddy and Me
Daddies are Special
Daddy's Girl
Daddy's Little Helper
Every Mother is a Working Woman
Father by Marriage
Father's Day Fun with the Daughters
Father's Day Fun with the Sons
Fun with Dad
Happy Dad's Day
Happy Father's Day
Happy Mom's Day
Happy Mother's Day
His Father, My Friend
I Am Man, Hear Me Snore
I Love My Kids
Just Me and My Ma
Just Me and My Pa
Like Daddy, Like Daughter
Like Father, Like Son
Like Mother, Like Daughter
Mom is the Best
Moms are Great!
Mom's Corner
Moms Make Memories
Mommy and Me
Mommies are Special
Motherhood is not for Wimps
My Dad, My Hero
My Dad's Cool!
My Heart Belongs to Dad
My Hero
My Mother, My Friend
My Other Father
One Classy Lady, My Mom
Shhhh...Dad's Sawing Logs
Superstar Dad

Superstar Mom
The Best Friend a Daughter Could Ever Have
The Proudest Daddy
Unconditional Love
World's Greatest Dad
World's Greatest Mom

....
....
....
....
....
....

GRANDPARENTS

A Classic
A Day with Grandpa
A Day with Grandpa Is Priceless
Best Gramps
Call Grandpa: 1-800-I-Want-It
Caution: Grandparents at Play
Grandmas are Great
Grandmas are Special
Grandma's Busy...Take a Number
Grandpas are Great
Grandpas are Special
Grandparents are Angels in Disguise
Grandparents Make Life Grand
Happiness is Having Grandchildren
Look Who's a Grandma Now!
My Grandma is the Grandest of All
My Grandpa Is The Grandest of All
My Hero
Priceless Wisdom
Snacks Taste Better At Grandma's House
The Lap of Luxury
The Nicest Nana
The Proudest Papa
The Timeless Beauty
They Don't Call Them Grand for Nothing
To Grandmother's House We Go
Two Proud Grandparents Live Here
With Age Comes Wisdom
World's Greatest Grandma
World's Greatest Grandpa

....
....
....
....
....
....

SISTERS & BROTHERS

A Brother is a Friend Forever
A Brother Understands
A Sister is a Friend Forever
A Sister Understands
A Sunshiny Day with a Good Friend
Brotherly Love
Brothers are a Special Gift
Brothers are Best
Brothers are Forever
Brothers by Heart
Brothers Since the Beginning...
Friends 'Til the End
Double Trouble
Friends from the Start
My Brother, My Friend
My Brother...My Best Friend
My Sister, My Friend

My Sister...My Best Friend

Oh Brother!

Peas in a Pod

Sisterhood is Powerful

Sisterly Love

Sisters are Forever

Sisters by Heart

Sisters Since the Beginning...
Friends 'Til the End

Two Peas in a Pod

You and Me, Buds Forever!

....

....

....

....

....

COUSINS

Cousins and Friends

Dozens of Cousins

Herd of Cow-sins

Kissin' Cousins

Kissing Cousins

My Cousin, My Friend

....

....

....

....

....

GRANDCHILDREN

Grandchildren Make Life Grand

Grandchildren Put the Magic Back into Life

Grandkids Keep Hearts Young

Grandma's Little Angel

Grandma's Little Heartthrob

Grandma's Sweetheart

Grandpa's All Star

Grandpa's Delight

Grandpa's Little Angel

Grandpa's Sidekick

My Grandchildren are
the Grandest of Them All

They Don't Call Them Grand for Nothing

....

....

....

....

....

PRE-BABY

Already Adorable

Anticipation

False Alarm

Great Expectations

Here I Am!

It's Almost Time...

Labor and Delivery

Lady in Waiting

Look Out World, Here I Come!

Make Room for Baby

Our Growing Family

Peek-a-Boo We See You

She's About to Pop

Sneak Preview

The Big Day

Ultrasound

Under Construction

What a Belly!

Womb with a View

Wow, We're Pregnant!

....

....

....

....

....

BABY

A Blessing

A Blessing from Above

A Bundle of Joy

A Child is God's Greatest Gift

A Child of God

A Gift from Above

A Gift from God

A Labor of Love

A New Bundle of Joy

A Perfect Angel

A Special Hug for You, from Me

A Star Is Born

A Sweet Miracle

A Whole New World

Absolutely Adorable

Isn't I Great?

All Boys

All Dolled Up

All Girls

All I Want to do is Chew Chew Chew

Amazing Baby

An Answered Prayer

As Free as a Bird

Babies Make the World a Happier Place

Babies Put Magic in our Lives

Baby Boy

Baby Girl

Baby Love

Baby on Board

Baby on the Move

Baby Steps

Baby Talk

Bald is Beautiful

Bare Bottom

Bear Hug

Beautiful Dreamer

Born in the USA

Born to be Wild

Born to Cause Trouble

Bouncin' Baby Boy

Bouncin' Baby Girl

Bouncing Baby Boy

Bouncing Baby Girl

Boy Meets World

Broadway Baby

Bubble Bath

Bundle of Joy

Bundle of Love

Catchin' Some Zzzz's

Cherish the Moment

Clean as a Whistle

Close Your Sleepy Little Eyes

Counting Sheep

Cruisin'

Cuddle Buddies

Cuddle Bugs

Cuddles and Kisses

Cute and Cuddly

Cute as a Bug

Cute as a Button

Cute-N-Cuddly
Cutie Pie
Don't Cry Baby
Dream Baby
Drool is Cool
Eating Again?
First Impressions
First Steps
Friday's Child is Loving and Giving
Future Champion
Future Star
Girl Meets World
God Bless This Child
God's Greatest Gift
Got Milk?
Great Things Come in Small Packages
Growing Pains
Here I Am!
He's Only Recharging
Heaven Sent
Hello World, Here I am!
Hello Little One
How Do I Look?
How Wonderful!
Hush Little Baby
I am a Child of God
I Couldn't Be More Lovable if I Tried
I Have Arrived
I Have Arrived at Last
I Think I Can, I Think I Can, I Can (crawling & walking)
I'm a Keeper
I'm a Miracle
I'm a Real Handful
I'm Awake, Let's Play
I'm Just "Plane" Cute
I'm Not Always An Angel
I'm Too Cute for Words
Introducing the World's Most Beautiful Baby
It's a Baby Boy
It's a Baby Girl
It's a Bouncing Baby Boy
It's a Bouncing Baby Girl
It's a Boy!
It's a Girl!
Just Arrived
Just as Cute as Can Be
Let the Good Times Roll
Life Is Full of Firsts
Lil' Darlin'
Lil' Stinker
Little Angel
Little Charmer
Little Darlin'
Little Sprout
Look at that Face
Look Daddy!
Look Mommy!
Look Out World, Here I Come!
Look What Heaven Sent
Look What I Can Do!
Look Who's Talking
Miles of Smiles
Miracle Baby
Miracles Happen Everyday
Mmm, Mmm Good!
Monday's Child is Fair of Face
Nap Time
New Kid on the Block
New Life
New Life Begins

New Life...New Love
New Rookie on the Block
Nighty Night
Now I Lay Me Down to Sleep
Oh Baby, You're Beautiful
Oh, Baby!
Our Baby Angel
Our Bundle from Heaven
Our Dream Come True
Our Little Angel
Our Little Love Bug
Our Little Princess
Our Little Son-shine
Our Little Sweetie
Our Little Treasure
Our New Arrival
Our Perfect Angel
Our Pride and Joy
Our Shining Star
Our Special Delivery
Peek-a-boo!
Perfection
Practice Makes Perfect
Precious Angel One
Precious Little One
Pretty as a Picture
Puppy Love
Ring Around the Rosie
Rock-a-Bye Baby
Rub a Dub in a Tub
Saturday's Child Works Hard for a Living
See How They Grow
Shh... Babies Sleeping
Shh... Our Little Angel is Sleeping
Simply Irresistible
Sleeping Beauty
Sleepy Time
Snakes and Snails and Puppy Dog Tails
Snips 'n' Snails
Snug as a Bug in a Rug
So Big!
Sooooooo Big!
Special Delivery
Splash, Splash, I Was Taking a Bath
Squeaky Clean
Sugar 'n Spice
Sunday's Child is Full of Grace
Sweet as Can Be
Sweet Dreams
Sweet Little Thing
Teething is a Real Pain
Ten Tiny Fingers
Ten Tiny Toes
Thank Heaven for Babies
The Apple of My Eye
The Love of Our Lives
The Pitter Patter of Little Feet
The World's Best Baby
There's a First Time for Everything
This is How an Angel Sleeps
This Little Piggy...
Thursday's Child has Far to Go
Time for a Nap
Tiny Blessings Make Life a Joy
Tiny Bubbles
Too Adorable
Too Cute for Words
Touched by Love
Tuesday's Child is Full of Grace
We Made a Wish and You Came True

Wednesday's Child is Full of Woe

Welcome Little One

Welcome Sweet Baby

Welcome to Our World

What a Babe

What a Miracle

When Do We Eat?

When You Wish Upon a Star

Yep, Ten Toes

You Were Worth Every C-O-N-T-R-A-C-T-I-O-N

You've Got Style Baby

You've Got the Cutest Little Baby Face

You Are My Sunshine

Yummy

....

....

....

....

....

....

TWINS

A Double Blessing

Copy Cats

Double Exposure

Double Trouble

How Many?

Like 2 Peas in a Pod

Me and My Womb Mate

Our Family Just Grew by Four Feet

Seeing Double

The More, the Merrier

Twice Blessed

Twice the Fun

Two by Two

Two of a Kind

....

....

....

....

TRIPLETS

How Many?

Like 3 Peas in a Pod

Me and My Womb Mates

Terrific Triplets

The More, the Merrier

Three of a Kind

Three Times the Charm

Three's a Crowd

Three's Company

Thrice Blessed

Triple Trouble

....

....

....

....

CHILDREN

100% Cute Kid

A Child Enjoys Life's Simple Pleasures

A Child is God's Greatest Gift

A Child of All Seasons

A Little Bookworm

A Perfect Angel

Absolutely Adorable

Accessorize Yourself

Ain't I Cute?

All Dolled Up
All Grown Up
All Washed Up
Another Day, Another Play
As Cuddly as a Teddy Bear
As Good as Gold
As Snug as a Bug in a Rug
Bathing Beauty
Bear-y Special
Bedtime Story
Bee-ing Cute
Best Dressed
Big Shot
Block Party
Born to Be Wild
Bubble Trouble
Busy as a Bee
Butterfly Kisses
Child's Play
Children are Angels
Children Make the World a Happier Place
Children Put the Magic in Life
Clowning Around
Come Out and Play
Cute as a Bug
Cute as a Button
Cute as Can Bee
Cute is My Middle Name
Cutie Pie
Daddy's Angel
Destruction Zone
Did You Say "Bath Time or Play Time"?
Discover Wild Life, Have Kids
Eating Again?
Entering the Kids Zone
Everyday Moments are Cherished Memories
Go, Go, Go!
Going, Going, Gone
Growing Like a Weed
Growing Pains
Growing by Leaps and Bounds
Growing, Growing, Grown
Hammin' It Up
He's Only Recharging
Hold On
How Do I Look?
How Do You Like Me Now?
I Couldn't Be More Lovable if I Tried
I Did It!
I Love Bath Time
I Think I Can, I Think I Can, I Can!
I'll Do Anything Once
I'm a Kissable Kid
I'm a Real Handful
I'm in Charge Here
I'm Not Always An Angel
I'm the Boss
Just Me and My Dad
Kids with Class
Kiddin' Around
Kids at Play
Kool Kid
Let's Eat
Like Father, Like Son
Lil' Honeybee
Little Boys are Special
Little Charmer
Little Girls are Special
Little Mr. Son-shine

Little Sprout

Little Stinker

Living Dolls

Look Out World, Here I Come!

Look What I Can Do

Lookin' Good

Love Ya Kiddo

Luv the Tub

Me and My Shadow

Measuring Up

Mmm, Mmm Good!

Mommy's Angel

Mommy's Little Angel

Munchie Time

Not a Baby Anymore

On the Go

Our Little Angels

Our Pride and Joy

Personality Plus

Pitter Patter

Playtime 101

Practice Makes Perfect

Puppy Love

Radical Dude

Rub a Dub Dub, Two Boys in a Tub

Rub a Dub in a Tub

So Big!

So Silly

Someone Beary Special

Splish Splash

Spoiled Rotten

Squeaky Clean

Step-by-Step

Story Time

Such a Charmer

Super Kid

Sweet as Honey

Thank Heaven for Little Boys

Thank Heaven for Little Girls

The Apple of Our Eye

The Chicken Pox Days

The Cute Kid on the Block

The Kid with a Million Faces

The Little Engine That Could

The Princess and the Peas

The World's Best Kid

There's Nothing Sweeter Than
the Pitter Patter of Little Feet

This is How it's Gonna Be

This Magic Moment

Too Adorable

Too Cute for Words

Tub Time

"Udderly" Adorable

Under Destruction

Use Your Imagination

Wet 'n Wild

When I Grow Up...

World's Best Kid

Yield for Play

You are My Son-shine

You've Got the Cutest Little Baby Face!

Yummy

....

....

....

....

....

....

GIRLS & BOYS

100% Boy
100% Girl
A Chip Off the Old Block
All Boy
All Dolled Up
All Dressed Up and No Place to Go
All Dressed Up... Where Do We Go?
All Girl
Backyard Boys
Boy Meets World
Boy Power
Boys' Night Out
Boys are Us
Boys Rule!
Boys Will Be Boys
Caught Red-Handed
Caution: Boys at Play
Daddy's Girl
Gimme a Hand, Please
Girl Power
Girl Talk
Girls' Night Out
Girls Just Want to Have Fun!
Girls Rule!
Girls Will Be Girls
Glamour Girl
Hello Handsome
Hello Mr. Handsome
I'm a Real Handful
It Must Be A Guy Thing
It's a Girl Thing
It's a Guy Thing
Living Dolls
No Boys Allowed
No Girls Allowed
Oh, Boy!
Our Little Prince
Our Little Princess
Our Princess
Prince
Princess
Pure Boy
Pure Girl
Rough and Tumble
Sassy
So Handsome
So Many Girls, So Little Time
Sugar and Spice and Everything Nice
Tomboy

....
....
....
....
....
....

GIRLFRIEND & BOYFRIEND

A True Romantic
Boy Meets Girl
Crush
Cute Couple
My One and Only
Opposites Attract
Puppy Love

....
....
....
....
....
....

MEN

100% Macho Man
A Good Man is Hard to Find
A Jack of All Trades
Certified Stud Muffin
Handsome Hunks
It Must Be a Guy Thing
It's a Guy Thing
King Couch Potato
Man of the Hour
Me and My Girl
Real Men Do Ask for Directions
Real Men Do Cook
Real Men Do Housework

....

....

....

....

....

FRIENDS

2 Peas In a Pod
Best Buddies
Best Buds
Best Friends
Best Friends Always
Bestest Buddies
Buddy to Buddy
Buds
Double the Bubbles, Double the Fun
Fabulously Fun Friends
Forever Friends
Friend to Friend
Friends are Forever
Friends Forever
Friends from the Start
Friends See Heart to Heart
Friends Through Thick and Thin
Friends are the Essence of Life
Friendship Hits the Spot
Friendship in Bloom
Friendship is Fabulous!
Friendships Grow
Friends to the End
Gallery of Good Friends
Glad We're Friends
Kindred Spirits
Love One Another
Make a Friend Today
Me and My Shadow
My Circle of Friends
One in a Million!
Rainbow of Friendships
So Glad We're Friends
The Best of Friends, The Best of Buddies
Three's Company
Treasured Friends
Two of a Kind
Two Peas in a Pod
Two's Company
World's Greatest Friends!
Yakity-Yak
You and Me, Buds Forever
You Make Me Smile
You're the Best!

....

....

....

....

....

artwork from book #09700

Celebrations & Events

PARTIES & CELEBRATIONS

A Party Fit for a King
Block Party
Born to Party
Eat, Drink and Be Merry
It's a Party
It's My Party
It's Party Time
It's Time to Celebrate
Let's Party
Parties are Wonderful
Party Animal
Party Boy
Party Girl
Pizza Party
The Life of the Party
The More the Merrier

....

....

....

....

....

BIRTHDAY

"40" Happens (replace with other years)
2-riffic!
A Gift from The Heart
Age Doesn't Matter
Age is Only a Number
Aged to Perfection
An Oldie
An Oldie but Goodie
Antique Person
Bear-ly ___ Years Old
Bearly One Year Old
Big Birthday Bash
Big Things Come in Small Packages
Birthday Bash
Birthday Boy
Birthday Celebration
Birthday Girl
Birthday Greetings
Birthday Time
Born to Party
Celebrate Like Crazy!
Classified Information
Fantastic Fours
Forever Young
Forever Young in Spirit
Fun Being One (fill in with other ages)
Fun, Feisty and 50
Golden Oldie
Happy Day
Have a Dino-mite Birthday
Hip-Hip Hooray
I'll Have My Cake and Eat It Too
I'm Too Young to be This Old
It's Fun to Be One (fill in with other ages)
It's Party Time
It's the Big ____ (fill in with age)
It's the Big One
Just for You

Let's Celebrate

Let's Party

Look at Me, I Am Three (fill in with other ages)

Look Who's _____ (fill in with age)

Make a Wish

Me 40? I Demand a Recount!

Natural Aging Woman

Oh Dear, Another Year!

Old Geezer

Older Than Dirt

One is Wonderful

Over the Hill

Parties are Wonderful

Party Animal

Presents, Presents Everywhere

Ready, Set, Blow

Real Quality and Style

Silly Sixes

Simply Seven

So Many Candles, So Little Cake

So Many Presents, So Little Time

Still Young at Heart

Surprise!

Sweet Sixteen

Terrific Twos

The Big "___" (fill in with age)

The Big, Big Day

The Big One (fill in with other ages)

The Birthday Boy

The More Candles, the Bigger the Wish

The Parties are Wonderful

The Party's Here

The Perfect Gift

Thrilling Threes

Toasting Golden Moments

Too Old to Care

We're Celebrating You!

Wishes Do Come True

With Age Comes Wisdom

You're How Old?

You're Only Young Once

....

....

....

....

....

....

WEDDING

A Celebration of Love

A Dream Come True

A Kiss for Luck

A Life of Love We Will Have

A Match Made In Heaven

A True Romantic

Ain't Love Grand?

Always and Forever

And the Story Begins

And They're Off!

Be My Love

Bless You Two

Bubble Farewell

Celebration of Love

Cute Couple

Ever Together

Everlasting Love

Fairy Tales Do Come True

Forever

Forever and Ever

Get Me to the Church on Time

Goin' to the Chapel...

Happily Ever After

Happily Married
Hearts for Two
Here Comes the Bride
Honeymoon Sweeties
I Do
I Do! I Do! I Do!
I'll Love You Forever
It's Our Special Day
Just Hitched
Just Married
Look Who's Family Now
Love at First Sight
Love Birds
Love for All Time and Eternity
Love Grows When Shared
Love In Bloom
Love is Everlasting
Love is in the Air
Love Makes Life Complete
Lovebirds
Made for Each Other
My Best Friend, My True Love
My Knight in Shining Armor
My Love
My One and Only
New Beginnings
Now and Forever
Once Upon a Time...
Our Wedding
Radiant Faces of Love
Sealed with a Kiss
Sharing our Joy Together
Sharing Sweet Memories Together
She Loves Me, She Loves Me Not, She Loves Me
The Life of Love
The Love of My Life
The Wedding Party
This Magic Moment
To Have and to Hold
To Thee with Love
Today, I Marry My Best Friend
Today, Tomorrow, Always
Together Forever
Together We Stand
True Love
Two Hearts As One
Two Hearts Shall Be As One
Two Hearts Shall Beat as One
Two Hearts Shall Become One
Two Hearts United in Love
Unconditional Love
United in Love
We're in it Together
We've Only Just Begun
Wedding Bells
Wedding Bells Ring
With This Ring, I Thee Wed
World's Happiest Couple
Young Love

....

....

....

....

....

....

ANNIVERSARY

___ Happy Years (fill in with number of years)

___ Years and Still Going Strong
(fill in with number of years)

A Life of Love

A Match Made In Heaven

Everlasting Love

Happily Married After All These Years

Happy Yesterdays, Happier Tomorrows

Love Birds

Precious Memories

Still Going Strong After All These Years

Then and Now

Through the Years

Together Forever

....

....

....

....

....

ENGAGEMENT

A Night to Remember

Always and Forever

Breathtaking

Cherish the Moment

Cute Couple

Engaged

Engaged At Last

I said "Yes"

I Thought He'd Never Ask

I Thought You'd Never Ask

This Magic Moment

YES

....

....

....

....

....

RETIREMENT

Enjoy Life

Finally!

Happy Retirement

Hello Pension, Goodbye Tension

I Thought This Day Would Never Come

I'm Out of Here!

It's Finally Here

Now What?

Professional Tourist Here I Come

Retired, but not Tired

The Great Escape

Time for a Little R&R

Time Off for Good Behavior

Well Deserved

What Will They Do Without Me?

....

....

....

....

....

BAPTISM / DEDICATION / CHRISTENING

A Blessing

A Child of God

Our Child of God

Sunday's Child of God

....

....

....

....

....

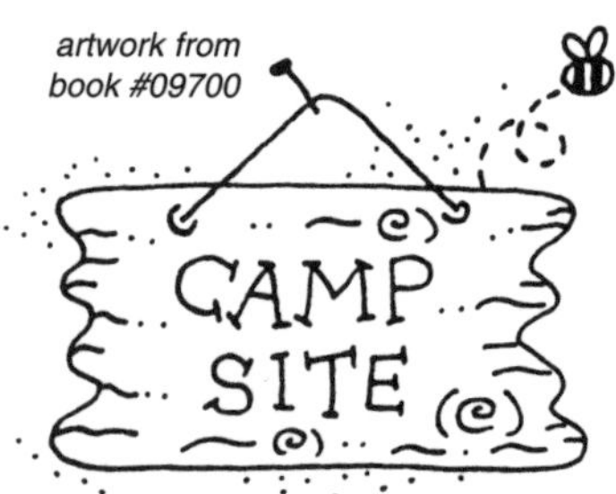

Vacation, Travel & Fun

VACATION TIME

A Family Retreat
A Land of Imagination
A Mountain Retreat
Adventure Time
Along for the Ride
Are We There Yet?
Away We Go
Begin the Journey
Beginning Our Journey
Exploring
Family Time
Family Trip
Homeward Bound
How Much Longer?
Miles of Smiles
Off We Go!
On The Road Again
On the Road...
On the Trail to Fun
Our Escape
Our Paradise
Paradise
Passport to Happiness
Professional Tourists
Rest and Relaxation
Road Trip
Run for the Border
Summer Vacation
The Great Escape
The Ride of My Life
The Time of Our Lives
This Sure Beats Work
Tourists
Vacation Genius at Rest
Vacation or Bust
We May Never Come Back Again
What A Joy Ride This Is
World Travelers

....

....

....

....

....

AIRPLANES

Aim High
First Flight
Flying High
Leaving on a Jet Plane
Up, Up and Away
What a Beautiful Country We Live In!
What a Flight!

....

....

....

....

BOATS

Ahoy
Anchors Away
Don't Rock the Boat
Row, Row, Row Your Boat

Sail Away
Ships Ahoy

....

....

....

....

CRUISE

Ahoy
All Aboard!
Anchors Away!
Away We Go
Aye, Aye Captain
Bon Voyage
Cruisin'
Cruisin' Along
Dining Delights
My Ship Has Finally Come In
"Ships" Ahoy

....

....

....

....

CIRCUS

Clowning Around
Lions and Tigers and Bears... Oh, My!
The Greatest Show on Earth
Under the Big Top

....

....

....

....

AMUSEMENT PARK

A Land of Imagination
Around and Around We Go
Hang On
Hang On Tight!
Let's Do It Again
Merry-Go-Round
Never Again
Up and Down We Go

....

....

....

....

PARK/PLAYGROUND

A Day in the Park
A Picnic in the Park
A Walk in the Park
At the Park
Higher! Higher!
Just a Swingin'
King of the Sandbox
King of the Playground
Play Day
Slide into Summer
Sliding Through Life
Slip Slidin' Away
Up, Up, and Away

....

....

....

....

BEACH OR SWIMMING

A Beautiful Day for the Beach
A Day at the Beach
A Seashell Search
A Splashin' Good Time
Bare Feet
Bare Feet and Fancy Feet
Bathing Beauties
Bathing Beauty
Beach Babes
Beach Babies
Beach Bum
Beach Bum Buddies
Beach Fun
Bikini Babe
Castles in the Sand
Catch a Wave
Catchin' Some Waves
Cool Fun in the Sun
Dive In
Down by the Sea
Down by the Seashore
Feelin' Crabby
Fun in the Pool
Fun in the Sun
Fun on the Seashore
Getting Wave Reviews
Jewels of the Sea
Life's a Beach
Little Mermaid
Makin' Waves
Official Beach Bum
Paradise
Pool Fun
Pool Time
Seashore Memories
Soakin' Up Some Rays
SPLASH!
Splish Splash
Squeaky Clean
Stay Cool
Staying Cool in the Pool
Super Soaked!
Superstar Swimmer
Sun ASAP!
Surf & Sand
Surf's Up!
Swims Like a Fish
The Beach
The "Bear" Necessities
The Beauty of the Beach
The Prince and His Castle
Tropical Fun!
Under the Sea
Unofficial Beach Bum
Watch Me!
Wet 'n Wild

....

....

....

....

....

....

CAMPING & THE OUTDOORS

Adventure Fun
Around the Fire
Back to Basics
Back to Nature
Camping is Life
Camp-o-rama
Camping Out
Candid Camping

Climb Every Mountain
Fresh Air
Great Adventure
Happy Campers
Life at its Best
Moonlight Madness
Nature Boy
Nature Center
Nature Girl
Nature's Beauty
On the Trail to Fun
Our Neck of the Woods
Outdoor Fun
Roughin' It
RV Adventures
S'more Camping
S'more Good Times
S'more Stories
Setting Up Camp
The Good Life
The Great Outdoors
The Simple Life
This is the Life
Under the Stars

....

....

....

....

PICNIC & COOKOUTS

A Family Tradition
A Taste of Summer
Backyard BBQ
Backyard Bash
Backyard Burgers
Backyard Cookout
Boy Meets Grill
Get Fired Up
Life is a Picnic
Life's No Picnic
No If's, Ants or Bugs About It
Picnic in the Park
Picnic Time
The Grill of Your Life

....

....

....

....

ZOO

A Zooper Day
After a While, Crocodile
Doing the Zoo Thing
Feedin' Time at the Zoo
Grizzly
G-R-O-W-L
It's a Jungle Out There
Lions and Tigers and Bears...Oh, My!
Monkeyin' Around
Our Trip to the Zoo
Petting Zoo
See Ya Later, Alligator
Welcome to Our Zoo
Welcome to the Zoo
What a Zoo!

....

....

....

....

All the Happy Holidays

NEW YEAR'S

A Big End to a Big Year

A Great Start for a New Year

Bringing in the New Year

Celebrate Good Times

Celebrating the New Year

Celebration

Good Times are Here to Stay

Happy ____ (fill in with the year)

Out with the Old, In with the New

Ringing in the New Year

The Future Looks Bright

....

....

....

....

....

VALENTINE'S DAY

A Day of Love

Be Mine

Be My Cupid

Be My Love

Be My Valentine

Happy Love Day

Happy Valentine's Day

Here's My Heart

Hugs and Kisses

Hugs are for Sharing

Love Potion No. 9

My Favorite Valentine

My Valentine

Sealed with a Kiss

S.W.A.K.

Sweet Valentine

Thanks Cupid!

To Thee with Love

Valentine Greetings

....

....

....

....

....

ST. PATRICK'S DAY

Best O'Luck

Feelin' Irish

Happy St. Patrick's Day

Lil' Leprechaun

Our Little Leprechaun

The Luck of the Irish

Top of the Morning

....

....

....

....

....

EASTER

An Egg-stra Fun Day

An Egg-stra Special Easter

Bunny Crossing

Carrot Patch

Easter Corner

Easter Egg Hunt

Easter Fun

Easter Greetings

Easter Traditions

Easter's on it's Way!

Egg-specially Cute

Eggs-treme Fun!

Everybunny is a Star

Everybunny Loves Me

Give a Cheer, Easter is Here!

Happy Easter

Happy Hoppers

He is Risen!

He Lives!

Hippity Hoppity, Easter Time is Here!

Hop on In

Hopping Down the Bunny Trail

Hoppy Easter

I Love Easter!

Somebunny Cares

Somebunny Loves Me

The Hunt is On

There's Nobunny Like You

You're Egg-cellent

....

....

....

....

....

4TH OF JULY & PATRIOTIC

100% Pure American

A Festive Fourth

All-American

All-American Kid

America, You're Beautiful

As American As Apple Pie

Born in the USA

Dyn-o-mite!

Freedom

God Bless America

God Bless the USA

Happy 4th of July

Happy Birthday America

Hatched in the USA

Hooray for the Red, White, and Blue

I Love America

Independence Day Picnic

It's a Grand Old Flag

Let Freedom Ring

Liberty

Made in America

My Country 'Tis of Thee

Old Glory

Proud to be an American

Red, White, and Blue

Stars and Stripes

Sweet Land of Liberty

The Land That I Love

This Land is Your Land

USA

We Had a Blast!

We Love America

....

....

....

....

....

HALLOWEEN

"Boo" from the Crew

A Bewitching Evening

A Haunting We Will Go

Boo to You!

Boo!

BOOtiful

Boo-tiful

Broom Parking... 5 cents

Candyland

Carving Out Fun

Carving Time

Casting A Spell

Caution: Ghost Crossing

Cutest Little Pumpkin in the Patch

Freakie Frankie

Fright Night

Ghost to Ghost

Goblin to Goblin

Happy Booday

Happy Halloween

Happy Haunting

Happy Haunts

Happy Haunts to You

Happy Howl-o-ween

I Love Being Witchy

I Love Halloween!

Lil' Pumpkin

Mom's Little Pumpkins

No Tricks, Only Treats!

Off We Go a-Haunting

Our Little Monsters

Pickin' Pumpkins

Picking and Grinning

Pumpkin Patch

Scare Up Some Love

Scaredy Cat

So Much Candy, So Little Time

Spooky Spider

Stop for a Spell

The Pick of the Crop

Trick or Treat

Trick or Treaters Welcomed

What Did You Get?

Witch to Witch

Witch Way?

Witch You Were There

Witchful Thinking

....

....

....

....

....

....

THANKSGIVING

A Day of Thanks

A Thanksgiving Feast

A Time for Thanks

As Stuffed as a Turkey

Be Ye Thankful

Bless This Food

Blessed are We

Bounteous Blessings

Bushel of Blessings

Count Your Blessings

Fall is Here!

Give Thanks

Giving Thanks

Gobble!

Happy Thanksgiving

Happy Turkey Day

Holiday Harvest

I'm Thankful for...

Let's Talk Turkey

Sharing the Food

Shower of Blessings

So Much to be Thankful For

Take Time to be Thankful

Thankful Days of Fall

Thankful for Family

Thanksgiving Bounty

Turkey Day

Turkey Time

We Are Gathered Here...

We Are Thankful For...

We Gather Together

We Give Thanks

We Thank Thee

What a Bunch of Turkeys

What a Turkey

....

....

....

....

....

....

CHRISTMAS

'Tis the Season

'Tis the Season for Love

'Twas the Night Before Christmas

100% Pure Christmas

A Gift of Love

A Holly, Jolly Christmas

A Jolly Old Soul

A Magical Mistletoe Moment

All Hearts Come Home for Christmas

All Wrapped Up

Beary Christmas

Believe in Magic

Berry Christmas

Berry Kissmas

Berry Merry Holly-days

Celebrate the Season

Children Put the Magic in Christmas

Christmas Blessings

Christmas Countdown

Christmas is on Its Way

Christmas Magic

Christmas Memories

Cookies are for Sharing

Countdown to Christmas

Country Christmas

Dear Santa

Do Not Open 'til Christmas

Do You Believe?

Down Home Christmas

Full of Christmas Love

Good Cheer

Goodies for Santa

Greetings

Greetings of the Season

Happy Birthday Jesus
Happy Christmas
Happy Holidays
Have a Jolly Christmas
Here Comes Santa
Ho! Ho! Ho!
Holiday Cheers
Holiday Greetings
Holiday Hugs to You
Holiday Memories
Holly Days
Home for the Holidays
I Love Christmas!
Jesus is Born
Jingle Bells
Jolly Christmas
Jolly Holidays
Joy to the World
Joy to You
Just Santa and Me
Keeping the Christmas Spirit
Kringle Crossing
Love...Joy...Peace...Hope
Magical Christmas
Merry Christmas
Naughty or Nice?
No Peeking
Noel
North Pole...Lost and Found
O Christmas Tree
O Holy Night
Oh Tannenbaum
Our Christmas Angel
Our Little Elves
Our Tree

Peace on Earth
Peace Unto the World
Reindeer Crossing
Rejoice
Santa Express
Santa Stops Here
Santa's Helper
Santa's on the Way
Santa's Workshop
Season's Greetings
Share Your Heart for Christmas
Sharing Our Christmas Together
Sharing Our Season Together
Silent Night, Holy Night
Simply Christmas Magic
So Many Toys, So Little Time
Surrounded with Joy
The Bearded Stranger
There's No Place Like Home for the Holidays
Toys, Toys, Everywhere
Tradition
Trimming the Tree
We Believe in Christmas
We Love Christmas
We're Dreaming of a White Christmas
Wishing you a Ho! Ho! Ho!
Wrapped in Love

....
....
....
....
....
....

Scrapbooking & Handiwork

SCRAPBOOKING

A Scrappin' Good Time
Capture the Memories
Crop 'Til You Drop
Crop Everything
Eek! Naked Pages!
For Generations to Come...
Gotta Scrap!
Good Til' the Last Crop
Help! I've Caught the Scrapbook Fever!
Made with Love
Ready, Set, Crop!
Saving Memories... Making New Ones
Saving Memories... Making Friends
Scrapaholic
Scrapaholics
Scrapbook Queen

....

....

....

HANDMADE

A Gift from the Heart
A Stitch in Time
C-R-A-F-T-Y
Cute as a Button
Handmade with Love
Look What I Made!
Sew Adorable
Sew Much Fun
Sew What!
You Keep Me in Stitches

....

....

....

HANDYMAN (also see Under Construction on page 64)

A Jack of All Trades
A Work in Progress
Caution: Men at Play
Caution: Men at Work
Construction Zone
Daddy's Big Helper
Fixer Upper
From Start to Finish
Grandpa's Fixin' Shop
Handyman
Home Improvements
If You Build It, They Will Come
Lil' Helper
Rome Wasn't Built in a Day
Room for Improvement
Sawdust Means Work in Progress
Tool Time
Under Destruction
What a Difference

....

....

....

artwork from book #09700

The Four Seasons

SPRING

April Showers
April Showers Bring May Flowers
Baskets of Flowers
Happy Spring
Hello Spring
I Love Spring
Love in Bloom
Spring Blossoms
Spring Breeze
Spring Fever
Spring Greetings
Spring Has Sprung
Spring into Life
Spring is in the Air
Spring Tulips
Springtime
The Voice of Spring
Think Spring
Welcome Spring

....

....

....

....

SUMMER

A Heat Wave
Barefoot and Fancy Free
Chill Out and Catch a Wave
Cool Summer Fun
Fun in the Sun
Here Comes Summer
Here Comes the Sun
Hot Fun in the Summer
Hot Fun in the Summertime
Hot Summer Days
Hot, Hot, Hot
I Love Summer
In the Good Old Summertime
Isn't Summer Fun?
Keeping Cool
Lazy Days of Summer
Lazy Summer Days
On the Sunny Side
Seasons in the Sun
Some Like it Hot
Summer Blossoms
Summer Break
Summer Breeze
Summer Days
Summer Delight
Summer Dreams
Summer Fun
Summer Girl
Summer Lovin' Girls
Summer's Joy
Summertime Blues
Summertime Fun

Super Summer Shots

Too Cool to be Hot

....

....

....

....

FALL

A Festival of Fall Colors

A Golden Fall

A Harvest of Memories

A Sign of the Season

Autumn Greetings

Autumn's in the Air

Autumn's Praise

Awesome Autumn

Be Thankful

Celebrating Fall

Changing Seasons

Color Me Autumn

Colorful Days of Autumn

Colors of Fall

Country Harvest

Crisp Autumn Nights

Crisp Days of Fall

Crisp Fall Air

Drifting Into Fall

Fabulous Fall

Fall "Leaves" Me Happy

Fall into Autumn

Fall Into Fun

Fall Memories

Fall's Coloring Book

Fall's Harvest

Fall's Here

Falling for You

Falling Leaves

Forever Fall

Happy Fall

Happy Harvest

Harvest Happenings

Harvest Happiness

Harvest of Happiness

Harvest of Love

Harvest Time

It's Fall

Keeper of the Crows

Love Those Leaves

On A Crisp Autumn Day

Pieces of Autumn

Piles of Fall Smiles

Piles of Fun

Playing in the Leaves

Pumkin' Patch

Shades of Autumn

Share the Harvest

Silly as a Scarecrow

The Cool Crisp Days of Autumn

Walking in a Fall Wonderland

Welcome Fall

....

....

....

....

WINTER

Brrrrr!!!

Chill Dude

Cold Days, Warm Hearts

Cold Hands, Warm Heart

Dashing Through the Snow

Frosty Friends

Happy Winter

If We Could Freeze Time

I Love Winter

Love Never Melts

Once There Was a Snowman...

Snowman Crossing

Snowtime

Snowy Days...Frosty Nights

Warm Toes and Tummies

Warmest Wishes

Welcome Snow

Winter Frolic

Winter Welcome

Winter Wonderland

Winter, Here We Come

....

....

....

....

artwork from book #09700

Weather

SNOW

B-L-I-Z-Z-A-R-D

Dashing Through the Snow

Frosty the Snowman

It's Snow Much Fun

It's Snow Time Folks

Let it Snow

Let it Snow, Let it Snow, Let it Snow

Our Little Eskimos

Snow Angel

Snow Baby

Snow Day

Snow Fun

Snow Much Fun

Snow Time

The Snowball Champion

Think Snow

....

....

....

....

RAIN

April Showers Bring May Flowers

Downpour

It's Raining Cats and Dogs

It's Raining, It's Pouring...

Look on the Bright Side

Our Rainy Day Sunshine

Rain, Rain, Go Away

Rain, Rain, Go Away,
Come Again Another Day

Raindrops Keep Fallin' on My Head

Rainy Day Fun

Showered with Love

Showers of Flowers

Singing in the Rain

Sprinkle...Sprinkle...Sprinkle

Sprinkled with Love

When It Rains, It Pours

....

....

....

....

RAINBOWS

A Rainbow is a Promise

Chasing Rainbows

Color Me Silly

Color My World

Look on the Bright Side

Over the Rainbow

Show Your True Colors

Somewhere Over the Rainbow

....

....

....

....

SUN

Feel the Burn

Fun in the Sun

Here Comes the Sun

Howdy Do Sunshine

Mr. Sun, Shine on Me

Seasons in the Sun

Soakin' Up Some Rays

The Light of My Life

You are My Sunshine

You Light Up My Life

....

....

....

....

SUNRISE/SUNSET

Breathtaking

Serenity

The Beginning of a New Day

The End of a Perfect Day

....

....

....

....

CLOUDS

A Ray of Sunshine on a Cloudy Day

Cloud Nine

Every Cloud Has a Silver Lining

Floating on a Cloud

....

....

....

....

Sports & Outdoor Activities

GENERAL

All Star Athlete
ALL STAR
Be a Winner
Certified Sports Nut
Champs!
Field of Dreams
For the Love of the Game
Future Hall of Famer
Go for the Gold
Go Team Go!
Go Team!
Go! Fight! Win!
Going the Distance
Having a Ball
In a League of Their Own
MVP
My Little All Star
Ouch!
Our Little Sports Nut
Our Team Mascot
Practice Makes Perfect
Score!
Sports Nuts
Superstar
Team Player
Team Spirit
The Champs
The Deadly Defense
The Sports Page
The Sweet Thrill of Victory
Three Cheers for Our Team!
V-I-C-T-O-R-Y
We're #1

....

....

....

....

ARCHERY

Bull's Eye
Right on Target
Sharpshooter
Straight as an Arrow

....

....

....

BASEBALL

All Star
All Star in Training
Baseball Fun
Batter Up
Having a Ball
Hit and Run
Home Run
Lil' Slugger
Little Slugger
Major Leagues, Here I Come
Our Little Slugger
Play Ball

Seventh Inning Stretch
Steeeerike!
Take Me Out to the Ball Game

....

....

....

....

BASKETBALL

All Star
Basketball Fun
Big Shot
Having a Ball
He Shoots, He Scores!
Hot Shot
MVP
MVP in Training
Nothing but Net
Slam Dunk!
Swoosh!
Team Spirit
Whoosh!

....

....

....

....

BICYCLING

Bike-a-thon
Happy Trails
Hittin' the Trail
If at First You Don't Succeed...
Look Mom, No Hands!
Practice Makes Perfect
Steady... Steady...
Steering Clear
Stop-n-Go
Trial and Error
Try, Try Again

....

....

....

BOXING

A Real Knockout
All Star
Down for The Count
Float Like a Butterfly, Sting Like a Bee
Putting Up A Fight

....

....

....

CHEERLEADING

Cheerleading Fun
Go! Fight! Win!
Go Team
Pom Pom Girls
Team Leaders
Team Spirit
We've Got Spirit, Yes We Do...

....

....

....

FISHING

Born to Fish, Forced to Work
Braggin' Rights
Caught Our Limit

Fish for Dinner

Fisherman on Duty

Fisherman's Delight

Fishermen Gather Here

Fishin' Fun

Fishing from Dawn to Dusk

Fishing Fun

Fishing is Life

Fishing Stories are Told Here

Fishing... It's a Reel Sport

Fishing...It's the Reel Thing

Gone Fishin'

Gone Fishing

Here Fishy, Fishy, Fishy

Hook, Line and Sinker

Hooked on Fishing

I'm a Keeper

I'm Hooked on Fishing

Look What I Caught

Reel Fun

Reel Relaxed

Something's Fishy

Sounds a Bit Fishy!

The 1st Reel Fish I Ever Caught

The Catch of the Day

There's Something Fishy Going On Here

Will Fish for Food

....

....

....

....

FLYING KITES

Aim High

Flying High

Go Fly A Kite

High In The Sky

Up, Up and Away!

....

....

....

....

FOOTBALL

All Star

Football Fun

MVP

MVP in Training

Quarterback Cutie

Super Bowl

Team Spirit

Touchdown!

....

....

....

....

GOLF

A Hole in One

Born to Golf, Forced to Work!

Bye Bye Birdie

Fore!

Golf is Life

Golfers Gather Here

Putting Around

Queen of the Green

TEErific

The Swinger

To Golf or Not to Golf?

GYMNASTICS

All Star

Have Balance in Your Life

It's All in the Landing

Perfect 10

Team Spirit

Tumblin'

HIKING

A Walk On The Wild Side

Climb Every Mountain

Happy Hikers

Happy Trails

Headed Down The Wrong Path

Hike It Up

Hiker's Haven

Hiker's Paradise

Hittin' The Trail

Nature Hike

On the Trail Again

Take a Hike

Trail of Good Times

HOCKEY

All Star

Cold As Ice

Goal!

He Shoots, He Scores!

Hockey Fun

Incredible on Ice

Kings on Ice

Our Goal is More Goals

Score!

Team Spirit

The Puck Stops Here!

HUNTING

Big Shot

Born to Hunt, Forced to Work

Bull's Eye!

Gone Hunting

Hunters Gather Here

Hunters Lead a Wild Life

Huntin' Buddies

Hunting Fun

Hunting Season

On the Hunt

Practice Makes Perfect

Sharpshooter

The Buck Stops Here

Will Hunt for Food

....

....

....

....

RAFTING

Man Overboard

Riding the Rapids

Row, Row, Row Your Raft

Running the River

....

....

....

SKATING

All Star

Gliding Through Life

Incredible on Ice

Kings on Ice

Roller Derby

Rollin' Along

Skate into Winter

Skating on Thin Ice

Slippin' and Slidin'

Smooth as Ice

....

....

....

SKIING

Hittin' the Slopes

It's Downhill from Here

Just Glidin' Through

On a Downhill Slide

Ready to Hit the Slopes

Skiing Through Life

Snow Bunny

Time to Hit the Slopes

Winter Wonderland

....

....

....

SOCCER

All Star

Gettin' Our Kicks

GOAL

Having a Ball

I Get a Kick Out of You

SCORE

Soccer Fun

Team Spirit

....

....

....

....

SURFING

Body Surfing

Catch a Wave

Getting Wave Reviews

Surf's Up

....

....

....

TENNIS

L-O-V-E

Game-Set-Match

King of the Court

Queen of the Court

Tennis Anyone?

Tennis is My Racket

....

....

....

TRACK/RUNNING

All Star

From Start to Finish

Going, Going, Gone

Have a Field Day

It Runs in the Family

Makin' Tracks

On Your Mark, Get Set, Go!

Ready, Set, Go!

Road Runner

Runnin' Wild

Running in the Wind

Run Like the Wind

Track Fun

....

....

....

....

VOLLEYBALL

All Star

Bump, Set, Spike!

Having a Ball

ROTATE

SPIKE!

Team Spirit

Volleyball Fun

....

....

....

....

WALKING

First Steps

Going, Going, Gone

Look Mom, No Hands!

Look Out World, Here I Come!

Put Your Best Foot Forward

Ready, Set, Go!

Step-by-Step

....

....

....

....

WRESTLING

A Fight 'Til The End

All Star

Down for the Count

PINNED

Putting Up A Fight

Rough and Tumble

Take Down

....

....

....

....

School Days

SCHOOL

ABC's and 123's

All Grown Up

Back 2 School

Back to School

Education is the Key

First Day of School

Future Doctor

Future Honor Student

Genius in Training

Getting Educated

Golden School Days

Grade School Days

Great Events of Kindergarten
(replace with other grades)

Head of the Class

High School Days

Honor Student in Training

If at First You Don't Succeed...

Making New Friends

Making Progress

Making the Grade

Middle School Days

Mommy Cried, I Played

My Favorite Subject

My First Day of School

Practice Makes Perfect

School Days

School Daze

School is Cool

School's Out for the Summer

School Pals

School Spirit

Senior Trip

Spring Break

Star Student

Super Kid

Try, Try Again

When is Lunch?

When is Recess?

....

....

....

....

....

TEACHERS

"A" is for Apple

A+ Teacher

I Love My Teacher

Kids are My Business

Kids Color My World

Teach from the Heart

Teachers are Special

Teachers Have Class

Teachers Make a Difference

Teachers Rule

Teachers Touch Tomorrow

Teaching is a Work of Heart

The Dog Ate My Lesson Plans

To Teach is to Love

You Can't Scare Me... I Teach School

....

....

....

....

....

TEENAGERS

All Dolled Up

All Dressed Up with No Place To Go

Attitude? What Attitude?

Back to School

Beauty Queen

Best Dressed

Boy Crazy

Classmates

Cool

Drama Queen

Driving Me Crazy

Feeling Groovy

Fresh and Funky

Future Scientist

Girl Talk

Glamour Girl

Groovy Gals

Hangin' Out

Heartbreaker

High School Memories

Hot Date

Hot Stuff

How Do I Look?

How Do You Like Me Now?

In Your Dreams!

Lookin' Good

My Favorite Subject

No Direction in Life

Pajama Party Pals

Party Girl

School is Cool

School Pals

Sleepover

Social Butterflies

Spoiled Rotten

Student of the Month

Student of the Week

The Ride of My Life

Totally

Totally Cool!

Up All Night

Whatever

Wheels at Last!

You've Got Style, Babe

....

....

....

....

....

APPLES

"A" is for Apple

As American as Apple Pie

Picking and Grinning

Teachers Cannot Live by Apples Alone

The Apple Doesn't Fall Far from the Tree
The Apple of My Eye
The Pick of the Crop

....
....
....
....

GRADUATION

All Grown Up
Beginning a New Journey
Believe in Yourself
Class of _____ (fill in with year)
College Bound
Congrats Grad!
Congratulations
Congratulations Graduate
Congratulations... You Made It!
Diploma Dazzler
Finally
Follow Your Dreams
Grad Night
Graduation Day
Happy Graduation
Hats Off to the Graduate
Hats Off!
I Did It!
I Thought This Day Would Never Come
If You Dream It, You Can Be It
Kindergarten Graduation
Now I Can Get A Real Job
Now What?
Opportunity Knocks
Pre-school Graduation
Reach for the Stars
Senior Graduate
The Future Looks Bright
The Graduate
The Scholar

....
....
....
....

ART

A Colorful Personality
A Work of Art
Beauty is in the Eye of the Beholder
Chalk One Up for _____ (fill in with name)
Color Me Silly
Color My World
Doodle-ing
Great Job!
Imagination
Look What I Did
Look What I Made!
Masterpiece
Pretty Scribbles
Scribble... Scribble... Scribble
Showing My True Colors
The Many Colors of _______ (fill in with name)
What a Mess!
What an Imagination

....
....
....
....

BUS

Bus Boy

Ridin' the Bus

The Wheels on the Bus
Go 'Round and 'Round

....

....

....

....

COLLEGE

Away to School

College Bound

Dorm Sweet Dorm

My Dorm Away from Home

Roommates

Roomies

$end Money

....

....

....

....

COMPUTERS

Computer Bug

Computer Wizard

Connecting...

Crash!

Help!

Hit Any Key. With What?

Little Computer Bug

My Favorites

Networking

Press Any Key. No! No! Not That One!

Tech Support is Just a Busy Signal Away

The Wild, Wild Web

To Continue, Strike Keyboard with Forehead

World Wide Web

You've Got Mail

....

....

....

....

PROM

A Night to Remember

All Dressed Up

Dancing the Night Away

Dazzling

Dream Date

Memories in the Making

Oh, What a Night

Perfect Couple

Prom Night Delight

....

....

....

....

Pets, Animals & Insects

GENERAL

Animal Lover
Animals are Beautiful People
God's Creatures
I Love My Pets
Our Four-Legged Family
Our Pets
Our Zoo
Party Animal
Petting Zoo
We Love Our Pets

....

....

....

....

ANTS

Ants in Your Pants
No If's, Ants or Bugs About It

....

....

BEAR

"Beary" Cute
A "Beary" Good Boy
A "Beary" Good Girl
As Cuddly as a Teddy Bear
Bear Hugs Given Here
Bear Hugs to You
Bear with Me
Beary Best Buds
Beary Christmas
Bear-y Special
Cute 'n Cuddly
Free Bear Hugs
Grin and Bear It
G-R-O-W-L
Happy Bearday
I Can "Bearly" Wait
I Love Bears
I Love You "Beary" Much
I Love You Honey
I Wish I Was a Teddy Bear
Please Bear with Me
Someone Beary Special
Stuffed with Love
The "Beary" Best of Friends
The Bear Necessities

....

....

....

....

BEE

Bee-ing Cute
Bee Yourself
Catching a Buzz
Cute as Can Bee
Don't Worry, Bee Happy
Honey Bee Happy

Just Bee-boppin Around
Lil' Honeybee
My "Bee-utiful" Kids
Sweet as Honey
The Queen Bee
To Bee or Not to Bee

....

....

....

....

BIRD

A Little Birdie Told Me
As Free as a Bird
Backyard Beauty
Birds of a Feather (flock together)
Bye Bye Birdie
Feathered Friends
Feed the Birds
Hatched in the USA
Home Tweet Home
Lovebirds
Tweet Dreams
Tweet Tweet
Up, Up and Away

....

....

....

....

BUGS

As Snug as a Bug in a Rug
Bug Catcher
Computer Bug
Creepy Crawly
Cute as a Bug
Don't Bug Me
Fashion Bug
Love Bug
No If's, Ants or Bugs About It

....

....

....

....

BUTTERFLY

As Gentle as a Butterfly
Backyard Beauty
Butterfly Beauty
Butterfly Kisses
Flitter, Flatter
Flutterby Butterfly

....

....

....

CATS

Attack Cat on Duty
Cat Nappin'
Cats are People Too
Cool Cat
Copy Cat
Crazy Cat
Fat Cat
Here Kitty, Kitty!
I Love Cats
I'm Impawsible
Look What the Cat Dragged In
M-E-O-W

Meowie Christmas

No Dogs Allowed

Pampered Puss

Playful as a Kitten

PURRfect

Purr-fect Pals

"Purr-fectly Sweet"

Pussy Footing Around

Pussycat with Purr-sonality

Scaredy Cat

Smarty Cat

The Cat's Meow

Tiger in Training

What's Mew?

Wipe Your Paws

....

....

....

....

CHICKEN

Chick-a-dee

Chicken Little

Cock-a-Doodle-Doo

Hey Chicky

One Sick Chick

Slick Chick

....

....

....

COW

Dairy Queen

Got Milk?

Lil' Cowpoke

Love One an Udder

Milk Does a Body Good

Milkin' it for All It's Worth

MOOre Milk Please

Nature's Lawn-mooer

Udderly Adorable

Udderly Delicious

....

....

....

DOGS

A Boy's Best Friend

A Mutt

Attack Dog on Duty

Bad to the Bone

Dog at Play

Dog Day Afternoon

Dog Days of Summer

Doggone Adorable

Doggone Cute

Doggone Good to T-bone

Friends Furr-ever

Go Dog Go

Hot Diggity Dog!

I Don't Do Fetch

It's a Dog's Life

It's a Dog's World

Lap Dog

Make No Bones About It... I'm Cute!

Man's Best Friend

No Bones About It

No Cats Allowed

Pampered Pooch

Puppy at Play

Puppy Love

Puppy Play

Snakes, Snails and Puppy Dog Tails

Spoiled Puppy

The Family Mascot

Top Dog

Will Work for Bones

Wipe Your Paws

....

....

....

....

DUCKS

Duck Soup

Just Ducky!

My Little Rubber Ducky

Quack, Quack, Quack

You Quack Me Up

....

....

....

FROG

Don't Worry Be Hoppy

Feelin' Froggy? Jump!

I May Be a Prince, You Never Know

Is This Leap Year?

Kiss Me...

Ribbit, Ribbit

So Many Frogs... So Few Princes

Toadly Hoppy

Welcome to Our Pad

....

....

....

HORSE

All the Pretty Little Horses

Giddy Up

Horse Play

Horse Sense

Horsin' Around

Round 'Em Up

Straight from the Horse's Mouth

Stubborn as a Mule

....

....

....

MICE

As Quiet as a Mouse

EEK!

Say Cheese!

....

....

....

MONKEY

Going Bananas

Hear No Evil, See No Evil...

Monkey Business

Monkey See, Monkey Do

Monkeying Around

....

....

....

PIG

Hammin' It Up

Hogs and Kisses

Hogwash

Hog Wild

Oink...Oink...Oink

Pig Sty

Pig Out and Be Thin

Piggyback

Porky

This Little Piggy

....

....

....

RABBIT

Bunny Crossing

Happy Hoppers

Hippity Hop

Hop on In

Hopping Down the Bunny Trail

Somebunny Cares

Somebunny Loves Me

Somebunny Special

Somebunny's Sleeping

There's No Bunny Like You

Warm and Wonderful

....

....

....

SHEEP

A "Sheep" Skate

Bless Ewe

Ewe Amaze Me

Ewe are Loved

I Love Ewe

Sheep Skate

....

....

....

SNAKES

Slitherin' Around

Here's the Ssssssstory...

Snakes, Snails and Puppy Dog Tails

Ssssssnakes

....

....

....

SPIDER

Eensy Weensy Spider

Itsy Bitsy Spider

Spooky Spider

....

....

....

WORM

Bookworm

Gone Fishin'

Squirmy Worm

The Early Bird Gets the Worm

The Early Worm Gets the Bird

Wiggle, Wiggle, Wiggle

....

....

....

Farming & Ranching

FARM

A Farmer's Work is Never Done
A Little Bit Country
Bumper Crop
Bushels of Fun
Country Gal
Down on the Farm
Farm Family
Farm Fresh
Farm Raised
Farmer's Tan
Farmhand
Farmyard Fun
Field of Dreams
Fresh from the Farm
Goodbye City Life
Having a Hay Day
Hay, There!
Hog Wild
Lil' Farmer
Old McDonald Had a Farm
On the Farm
Outstanding in His Field
Pure Country Gal
Pure Country Guy
The Heart of the Country
The Pick of the Crop
Were You Raised in a Barn?
Yee-Haw!

....

....

....

RANCH

Back in the Saddle Again
Chow Time
City Slicker
Cowgirl
Cowboy
Giddy Up
Happy Trails
How the West Was Fun
Howdy
Howdy Y'all
Howdy "Pardner"
Lil' Cowpoke
Little Cowpoke
Ranch Hand
Ready to Ride
Round 'Em Up
Saddle Up
Stick 'Em Up
The Best of the West
The Heart of the Country
The Wild, Wild West
Welcome to the Ranch
Westward Ho!
Yee-Haw!
Yippee-yi-a!

....

....

....

Food, Diet and Exercise

EATING

A Taste of Summer

All I Want to do is Chew Chew Chew

An Egg-stra Special Mess

Brain Freeze

Chocoholic

Chocolate Solves Everything

Chow Time

Eat, Drink and Be Merry

Eating Again?

Finger Lickin' Good

Food Fight!

Food!

Here's the Scoop

Hmmm...

I'll Have My Cake and Eat it Too

Indulge

I Need Chocolate

I Scream, You Scream,
We All Scream for Ice Cream!

Let's Eat

Let's Eat Cake

Life is a Bowl of Cherries

Mmm, Mmm Good!

Scrumdillitelyumpschous

So Much Candy, So Little Time

Spoil Yourself

Summer Sweets

Sweet Tooth

Sweets... a Basic Necessity of Life

Sweets for the Sweet

Sweets for the Sweetie

The Bottomless Pit

Udderly Delicious

What a Mess!

What's for Dinner?

Yumm...

Yummy

BAKING & COOKING

A Little Lovin' from the Oven

A Pinch of This... A Dash of That

As American as Apple Pie

Baked with Love

Canned with Love

Cookin'? What is That?

Cooking Up a Storm

Cutie Pie

Family Recipe

Family Tradition

Flour Power

From the Kitchen of _______ (fill in with a name)

Give Me Some Sugar, Baby

Grandma's Kitchen

Here's What's Cookin'

Hey, Good Lickin'

Home Cookin'

It Takes a Lickin'

Keeper of the Kitchen

Kiss the Cook

Lend a Helping Hand

Look What's Cooking

Made with Love

Mom's Kitchen

My Favorite Recipe... Eat Out

Secret Ingredients

Self Service Kitchen

Special Recipe

Sugar and Spice and Everything Nice

Sweet as Sugar

Sweetie Pie

The Best You've Ever Tasted

The Kitchen is the Heart of the Home

The Prize ________ (fill in with a food name)

The Taste Test

This Chick is Cookin'

We're Cooking Now

What's Cookin', Good Lookin'?

What's Cooking, Good Looking?

....

....

....

....

....

....

DIET & EXERCISE

Be Strong

Burnin' Calories

Commit to be Fit

Eat Now, Diet Later

Feel the Burn

Feeling Fit

Firm, Fit and Fabulous

Fit and Fabulous

Fit and Firm

Hard Body

Hard Body in Training

Huff! Huff! Huff!

Huffin' and Puffin'

Just Do it

Light as a Feather

Living Large

No Pain, No Gain

Pumped Up

Slim and Trim

Taste makes Waist

Think Thin

Through Thick and Thin

....

....

....

....

....

....

This 'n That

ACTING

Break a Leg
Center Stage
Drama Queen
Hollywood, Here I Come!
In the Spotlight
Lights, Camera, Action!
The Show Must Go On
Theater of Dreams
There's No Business Like Show Business

....

....

....

ANGELS

A Perfect Angel
An Angel Sleeping
Angel Eyes
Angel on Duty
Angels on Duty
Angels Watching Over Us
Children Can Be Such Angels
Daddy's Little Angel
Earth Angel
I Believe
I Believe in Angels
I'm No Angel
Mommy's Little Angel
My Guardian Angel
Our Baby Angel
Precious Angel
Sent from Above
Shh... Angel Sleeping
This Is What An Angel Looks Like

....

....

....

....

BATH TIME

All Squeaky Clean
Bubble Bash
Bubble Bath
Clean as a Whistle
I Love Water!
It's Bath Time!
Little Streaker
Look Who's in the Tub
Making a Big Splash
Mr. Clean
Naked Baby Alert!
Rub-a-Dub-Dub
Splish Splash, I Was Taking a Bath
Tiny Bubbles
Wet 'n Wild

....

....

....

....

BEDTIME (also see Sleeping on page 62)

Beautiful Dreamer
Catchin' Some Zzzzs
Counting Sheep
Don't Let the Bed Bugs Bite
Dream Baby
Dreamer
Future Star
Good Night
Hush Little Baby
Nap Time
Nighty-Night
Now I Lay Me Down to Sleep
Princess Sleeping
Rock-a-Bye Baby
Sleep Tight
Sleeping Beauty
Sleepy Time
Sweet Dreams
Time for a Nap
When You Wish Upon a Star

....

....

....

CAMERAS

A Picture is Worth a Thousand Words
A Picture is Worth a Zillion Words
Big Shot
Capture the Memories
Capture the Moment
Everyday Moments
Freeze Frame
Grin and Bear It
Hammin' It Up
Let's See What Develops
Lights, Camera, Action
Miles of Smiles
My Mug Shots
Picture Perfect
Picture This
Pretty as a Picture
Priceless...
Say "Cheese"
Show Us Those Pearly Whites
Shutterbug
Smile
Snapshot in Time
Snapshots of Time
Take It Already
The Big "Cheese"
The Many Faces of _______ (fill in with a name)

....

....

....

CHURCH & RELIGION

A Blessing
A Day of Grace
A Day of Rest
A Gift from Heaven
Count Your Blessings
Have Faith
Heaven on Earth
Heaven Sent
I Believe
Our Sunday Best
Shining Bright
Sunday's Child is Full of Grace

....

....

....

DEATH

Always Loved, Never Forgotten

An Angel Watches Over Us

Cherish the Memory

In Loving Memory

Keeping the Memory Alive

My Guardian Angel

Never Forgotten

Rest in Peace

Rest Peacefully

Unforgettable

We Miss You

....

....

....

DRIVING

A Classic

Are We There Yet?

Begin Your Journey

Driving Is So Much Fun

Driving Me Crazy

Driving Us Crazy

Going the Extra Mile

How Much Longer?

On the Road Again

Speed Racer

Stop-N-Go

Vroom! Vroom!

....

....

....

EYEGLASSES

20/20

Set Your Sights High

SPECtacular

Stay Focused

....

....

....

FIRE

Don't Play with Fire

Hot Stuff

Hot! Hot! Hot!

Up In Flames

Where's The Fire?

....

....

....

FIRSTS

I Think I Can... I Think I Can... I Think I Can

I'll Do Anything Once

Life Is Full of Firsts

The First Time Around

There's A First Time for Everything

....

....

....

FLOWERS & GARDEN

A Growing Love

A Perennial Favorite

All Things Grow in Love

All Things Grow with Love

An Annual Event

April Showers Bring May Flowers

Backyard Beauty

Blossomland

Crazy about Watermelon

Cultivate Love

Farm Fresh Vegetables

Flower Power

Freshly Picked with You In Mind

Friendship Garden

Friendship Grows

Friendship in Bloom

Garden Patch

Gardening Grows the Spirit

Gather Your Dreams

Gettin' Down and Dirty

Grow... Dang It!

Grow... Please!

Growing Like a Weed

Grown in Love

Harvest Love

He Loves Me, He Loves Me Not

Hello Sunshine

Home Grown

How Does Your Garden Grow?

I Dig the Earth

Keeper of the Garden

Let it Shine

Look What's Sprouting Up

Love Grows Here

Love in Bloom

Miracles Grow

My Garden

No Weeds Please

Our Garden

Our Little Gardener

Our Little Sprout

Pickin' and Grinnin'

Plant a Little Sunshine

Plant Manager

Scatter Seeds of Happiness

Secret Garden

Seedin' and Weedin'

Seeds of Kindness

Sow Seeds of Kindness

Spring Has Sprung

Stop and Smell the Roses

Sunflower Patch

The Pick of the Crop

This Garden is Grown with Love

Tiptoe Through the Tulips

Weed Eater

Welcome to My Garden

You are My Sunshine

....

....

....

....

GAMBLING

All Bets are Off

Born 2 Bingo

I'll Betcha

Let's Make a Deal

Life's a Gamble

Poker Face

Slot Machine Queen

The Luck of the Draw

....

....

....

BOY & GIRL SCOUTS

Always Prepare
Be Prepared
Make New Friends
Scouts Honor

....

....

....

HAIR

A Hair-Raising Experience
Bad Hair Day
Bald is Beautiful
Bed Head
Big Hairy Deal
Buzz, Buzz, Snip, Snip
Buzzzzz Cut
Check Out My New Do
Curly Locks
Just a Trim Please
Knotty But Nice
My 1st Haircut
On the Cutting Edge
Peach Fuzz
Snip...Snip...Snip

....

....

....

HAPPY

Clowning Around
Don't Worry, Be Happy
Good Times
Happy Days
Life's Just Peachy
Oh Happy Day
On Top of the World
Peachy Keen
Smile
What a Peach
You Make My Heart Smile

....

....

....

HOUSE & HOME

Cozy and Charming
Fixer Upper
Home is Where the Heart Is
Home Sweet Apartment
Home Sweet Home
House + Love = Home
Love Makes A House A Home
New Address, New Attitude
Our Dream House
Our Lil' Cottage
Our Lil' Home
Our Mansion
The American Dream
There's No Place Like Home
We've Moved

....

....

....

INJURY, ILLNESS & HOSPITAL

A Clean Bill of Health
A Picture of Health
All Better
All Stitched Up
Boo-Boo

Caught a Bug
EMERGENCY
First Aid
Homesick
In Sickness and in Health...
Laughter is the Best Medicine
Life is Fragile
Lookin' Good
Love Conquers All
Lovesick
Moanin' and Groanin'
My Boo-Boo
Never Mind, I'm Suddenly Feeling Better
Oh, My Aching...
OOPS!
OUCH!
Road to Recovery
Say "Ah"
Sick Chick
Tender Loving Care
The Road to Recovery
This Hurts Me More Than It Hurts You
This Won't Hurt a Bit
Time Heals All Wounds
What's Up, Doc?
You Keep Me In Stitches

....

....

....

INSPIRATIONAL

A Leap of Faith
Believe in Miracles
Bless This Home
Cheerful Giver
Cherish the Moment
Children are a Gift from God
Count Your Blessings
Enter with a Happy Heart
Expect a Miracle
Follow Your Dreams
From the Heart
Gather Your Dreams
God Bless This Home
God is Love
God Keeps His Promises
Heart to Heart
Help Lord, I'm in a Spot
Hug One Another
I Love My Family
Jump for Joy
Kindness Begins with Me
Life's Precious Moments
Live in the Moment
Love Warms the Heart
Moments to Share
Notice the Little Things
Perfect Harmony
Precious Moments Together
Reach for the Stars
Ready to Take on the World
Sharing Life's Blessings
Stop and Smell the Roses
Thank Heaven!
The Heart of the Home
Unconditional Love
You Are My Happiness

....

....

....

LOVE, KISSES & HEARTS

A Gift from the Heart
A Gift of Love
A Growing Love
A Kiss for Luck
A Life of Love
A Match Made in Heaven
A Mother's Love
A Work of Heart
All Things Grow with Love
Bitten by the Love Bug
Cheek to Cheek
Cuddles and Kisses
Embrace Life
Everlasting Love
Faith...Hope...Love
Follow Your Heart
Forever and Ever
He Loves Me, He Loves Me Not
Heart to Heart
Hearts Forever Entwined
Home is Where the Heart Is
Hugs and Kisses
I Only Have Eyes for You
I'm Coo-koo Over You
Live Well...Laugh Often...Love Much
Loads of Love
Love Begins at Home
Love Bugs
Love Conquers All
Love Goes on Forever
Love Grows Between Us
Love Grows When Shared
Love in Bloom
Love is a Hug
Love is Everlasting
Love is in the Air
Love is Kind
Love is Sharing
Love is the Best Gift of All
Love Lifted Me
Love Lives Here
Love Makes Life Complete
Love One Another
Love Warms the Heart
Love You
Made for Each Other
Moments of Love
My Eyes Adore You
My Heart and Soul
My Heart Belongs to You
My Knight in Shining Armor
My One and Only
Preserved with Love
Puppy Love is from Above
Reflections of His Love
Sealed with a Kiss
Share Your Heart
Smile, God Loves You
Snuggle Bug
Sprinkles of Love
SWAK
Tender Loving Care
The Love of My Life
Thoughts of You...
Totally Nuts About You
Touched by Love
True Love
Unconditional Love
Walking on Cloud Nine

Wrapped in Love
XOXOXOX
You Are My Sunshine
You Complete Me
You Have the Key to My Heart
You Light Up My Life
You Make My Heart Smile
You've Captured My Heart
Your Love is So Uplifting

....

....

....

MEMORIES

A Day to Remember
A Happy Memory Captured Forever
Capture the Memories
Cherish Old Memories
Cherish the Memories
Cherished Days
Everyday Memories
For Old Times Sake
Gallery of Good Memories
Gone But Not Forgotten
Heading Down Memory Lane
I Remember When...
Keeping The Memory Alive
Legacy Lane
Magical Memories
Memorable Moments
Memories are What Life is all About
Memories for a Lifetime
Memories in the Making
Memory Lane
Priceless...
Remember When...
Saving Memories One Page at a Time
Seems Like Yesterday
Special Memories
Thanks for the Memories
The Good Ol' Days
The Way It Was
These are the Times to Remember
Through The Years
Treasured Thoughts
Where Did The Time Go?

....

....

....

MESSY

A Little Dirt Never Hurt Anyone
Could Somebody Bring Me a Mop?
Getting Down and Dirty
Have You Ever Seen Such A Mess?
I'm a Mess
Lil' Pig
Look What I Did
Oops!
Pig Sty
This Little Piggy
Trashed
Uh-Oh!
What a Mess!
What's a Little Mud?
Yuck!

....

....

....

MILITARY

Above and Beyond

Our Hero

Proud to be an American

Proud to Serve

Rank and File

Stand at Ease

Wings of Victory

....

....

....

MISCELLANEOUS

I Don't Do Mornings

I Love Stress

Lord, Slow Me Down

Nobody's Perfect

T.G.I.F

....

....

....

MONEY

$$$$$

Big Spender

Cha-ching!

Deep in Debt

I Owe, I Owe, Off to Work I Go!

I'm Rich!

Moolah!

Ooh la la!

Penny Pincher

Right on the Money

Rolling in the Dough

The Buck Stops Here

Who Wants to be a Millionaire?

....

....

....

MUSIC, DANCE & SHOW BUSINESS

2 Left Feet

A Little Bit Country, A Little Bit Rock-n-Roll

A Rocking Good Time

A Star is Born

A Star Performance

Action!

Baby Grand

Bang! Clash! Bang!

Dance the Night Away

Dancers Have Happy Feet

Dancin' to a Different Beat

Encore!

Feel the Rhythm

First Recital

Footloose and Fancy Feet

I'm a Star!

I'm Here to Entertain You

I've Got Rhythm

Kick Up Your Heels

Let the Music Play

Lil' Drummer Boy

Music is Love

Music to My Ears

Perfect Harmony

Practice Makes Perfect

Practice... Practice... Practice

Put on Your Dancin' Shoes

Put Your Best Foot Forward

Rockin' and Rollin'

Rock-n-Roll

Sidekicks

Sounds of Music

Step-by-Step

Strike Up the Band

The Baby Boogie

The Star of the Show

Tiny Dancer

Twinkle Toes

Two Left Feet

We're Rockin' Now!

You've Got Rhythm

....

....

....

MOTORCYCLE

Born to Be Wild

Born to Ride

Me and My Hog

....

....

....

NEWSPAPER

Classified

Extra! Extra!

Extra! Extra! Read All About Me!

Front Page News

Have You Heard the Good News?

Making News

News Flash

Read All About It

Read All About Us

Special Edition

....

....

....

NOAH'S ARK

All Aboard!

Flooded with Blessings

Two by Two

....

....

....

REUNIONS

A Family Tradition

How Long Has it Been?

It's Been Way Too Long

Reunited After All These Years

Together at Last

....

....

....

SAD

Don't Worry... Be Happy

Sooo Sad

Sorrowful Day

Why the Long Face?

....

....

....

SHOPPING

Born to Shop
Let's Make a Deal
Material Girl
Shop 'Til You Drop
Shop-a-holic
Shopping is in Our Genes
Spending Spree
We Came, We Shopped, We Conquered

....

....

....

SLEEPING (also see Bedtime on page 53)

A Lullaby Moment
All is Calm
All Tucked In
As Snug as a Bug in a Rug
Bed Head
Counting Sheep
Early to Bed, Early to Rise
Follow Your Dreams
Life is but a Dream
May All Your Dreams Come True
Naptime
Nite Nite
Now I Lay Me Down to Sleep
Recharging
Shh... Angel Sleeping
Sleeping In
Sleepy Head
Sweet Dreams
Zzzzz

....

....

....

STARS

A Shining Star
A Star is Born
A Star Performance
Catch a Falling Star
I'm a Star!
Make a Wish...
My Little All Star
One in a Million
Our Shining Star
Reach for the Stars
Shoot for the Stars
Star Power
Starry, Starry Night
Stars in Your Eyes
SUPERSTAR
The Star of the Show
Twinkle, Twinkle Little Star
When You Wish Upon a Star...
Wish Upon a Star

....

....

....

TEETH

A Visit from the Tooth Fairy
No Cavities
Look What the Tooth Fairy Left
Loose Tooth
Show Us Those Pearly Whites
Sweet Tooth
Teething is a Real Pain
Tooth Fairy
"Toothless in Seattle"

....

....

....

TELEPHONE

Hello?

Phone Home

Ring...Ring...Ring

Say What?

What Did We Do Before Cell Phones?

What Did We Do Before the Telephone?

....

....

....

TIME

A Timeless Beauty

If We Could Only Freeze Time

Perfect Timing

The Passage of Time

Then and Now

Time After Time

Time Lapse

Time Out

Travel Back in Time

Wait a Minute

Well Worth the Wait

Where Did the Time Go?

....

....

....

TOILET & TOILET TRAINING

A King and His Throne

I'm a Big Boy Now

In Training

It's My Potty and I'll Cry if I Want To

Oops!

Who Needs a Diaper? Not Me!

....

....

....

TRAINS

All Aboard

Choo! Choo!

I Think I Can... I Think I Can... I Think I Can!

Imagination That Could

The Little Engine That Could

Welcome Aboard

....

....

....

TREE HOUSE

Home Away from Home

No Boys Allowed

No Girls Allowed

....

....

....

TROUBLE

Caught in the Act

Caught Red Handed

Here Comes Trouble

I Didn't Do It

I'm a Real Handful

Misbehavin'

Mischievous is My Middle Name

Oops!

Partners in Crime

Problem Child

The Devil Made Me Do It
The Scene of the Crime
They Call Me Trouble
Trouble is My Middle Name
Troublemaker
We Did It!
What a Little Angel!
Whoops!
Who Me?
Whose Idea Was This?
Yikes!

....

....

....

UNDER CONSTRUCTION

(also see Handyman on page 29)

A Jack of All Trades
Construction Zone
Dig It
If You Build It, They Will Come
Under Construction

....

....

....

VOLUNTEER

A Labor of Love
Changing Lives
Every Little Bit Helps
Lend a Helping Hand
Making the World a Better Place
Touching Lives

....

....

....

WORKING WORLD

A Hard Day's Work
A Labor of Love
All Work, No Play
Another Day, Another Dollar
Business as Usual
My Associates, My Friends
Opportunity Knocks
T.G.I.F
Waiting for the Weekend
Whistle While You Work
Working Together

....

....

....

WORLD

As the World Turns
It's a Small World
Joy to the World
Making the World a Better Place
Mother Earth
Oh What a Wonderful World
On Top of the World

....

....

....

WRECK

A Nervous Wreck
Just Call Me Crash
Oops!

....

....

....

LETTERING (more lettering on following page)

USE PROPER SPACING...

PROPER SPACING is NOT achieved by using a ruler to measure even spaces between letters!

CORRECT SPACING is done VISUALLY.

Print out the word you are using. We have chosen the word "LAND" for our example. Notice the spacing between the L and the A. Compare that with the space between the N and the D. These differences occur just because of the letter shapes. To make lettering beautiful, your eye must determine an EQUAL SPACE between each letter. Study the examples. It is something that becomes easier the more often you do it. At first you may have to trace, erase and then trace again...just to make your word look right.

L A N D

WRONG Shows measured spacing

LAND

CORRECT Example of visual spacing

LETTERING refer to instructions for proper spacing on previous page

a b c d e f g h i j

k l m n o p q r s

t u v w x y z ? !

1 2 3 4 5 6 7 8 9 0

A B C D E F G H I

J K L M N O P Q

R S T U V W X Y Z